TOEFL GRAMMAR GUIDE

23 Grammar Rules You Must Know To Guarantee Your Success On The TOEFL Exam!

Timothy Dickeson

TOEFL Grammar Guide – 23 Grammar Rules You Must Know To Guarantee Your Success On The TOEFL Exam!

ISBN-13: 978-1484046043

Table of Contents

Why You Need To Read This Book

If you are about to take the TOEFL exam soon, then you must review your grammar, especially the principles that are most commonly used in the TOEFL.

Did you know that your overall TOEFL score is weighed based on your grammar accuracy and use?

If you look at the scoring criteria that the TOEFL evaluators use, you will see an element which covers at how well you use the different grammar principles and how accurate you use them.

So, apart from learning how to develop high scoring answers in the writing and speaking sections and understanding the correct strategies for answering the reading and listening questions, you MUST correct your grammar to ensure you achieve a high score.

This book has been especially written to help you <u>review</u>, <u>understand</u> and <u>correct</u> the most common grammar rules used in the TOEFL exam.

For each TOEFL grammar rule, you will learn:

- The fundamental use of the rule
- How to use it (with simple examples and explanations)
- When to use it
- Signalling words

- Important tips

So, if you are about to take the TOEFL exam soon, you MUST NOT FORGET to review your grammar, because it could mean the difference between achieving the score you need or not!

TOEFL Grammar Rule No.1 - *Simple Present*

Description

Simple present is used to express the idea that an action is continuously repeated or an action that happens usually. The action can be a daily event, a habit or something that often happens.

How To Use It

Structure: VERB + s/es (in the third person)

Example: "She <u>speaks</u> English", "I <u>like</u> salad", "They don't <u>like</u> fish"

Explanation: The Simple present is easy to conjugate with <u>Regular</u> verbs because they all finish in the same form. For example, the verb "to eat".

Subject	Conjugated Verb
I	Eat
You	Eat
She/He	Eat<u>s</u>
We	Eat

You (plural)	Eat
They	Eat

However, <u>Irregular</u> verbs do NOT follow this pattern. For example, the verb "to be":

Subject	Conjugated Verb
I	Am
You	Are
She/He	Is
We	Are
You (plural)	Are
They	Are

When To Use It

Here are the 4 ways to use it:

- Repeated actions > "I <u>go </u>to the gym on Monday and Thursday"
- Permanent states > "The Sun <u>rises</u> in the morning""
- Scheduled events in the near future > "The plane <u>leaves</u> at 6 am tomorrow"
- Now (non-continuous) > "I <u>am</u> here now"

Signalling Words

Frequency Adverbs: Always, never, sometimes, Once/Twice a week/month, etc.

Important Tips

Many people make the mistake of combining the present continuous with the simple present.

These forms are **INCORRECT**:

> "She running fast"

> "I am go to the mountains"

These forms are **CORRECT**:

> "She is running fast"

> "I am going to the mountains"

TOEFL Grammar Rule No.2 - *Simple Past*

Description

Simple past is used to express an action that started and finished at a specific time in the past.

How To Use It

Structure: VERB + ed (regular verbs), or other forms for irregular verbs

Example: "She spoke English", "I liked the salad", "They didn't like the fish".

Explanation: Below it is shown how the verb changes for a Regular verb and for an Irregular verb:

Regular verb (Simple Past)

Verb – "to talk"

Positive	Negative	Question
I talked	I did not talk	Did I talk?

Irregular verb (Simple Past)

Verb – "to speak"

Positive	Negative	Question
I spoke	I did not speak	Did I speak?

When To Use It

Here are the 5 ways to use it:

- Completed action in the past > "Last year, she travelled to Japan"
- A series of completed actions > "We talked on the phone, then met for coffee and later went to the movies"
- Duration in the past > "They lived in Brazil for 5 years"
- Habits in the past > "I never played the piano"
- Past facts or generalisations > "I was a shy child"

Signalling Words

Yesterday, 2 minutes ago, in 1990, the other day, last Friday, etc.

Important Tips

Words ending in "ed" are often pronounced incorrectly, simply because people aren't aware of the following rules.

Rule 1: All words that have the last consonant as a "t" or "d" before "ed" must be pronounced with the "ed" as a separate syllable.

For example: (Pronunciation with syllables)

- Translated – (Trans – la – ted)
- Needed – (Nee – ded)
- Deposited – (De – pos – i – ted)

Rule 2: All other words that have the last consonant other than "t" or "d" before "ed" must be pronounced without the "e", and the "d" is combined with the previous syllable.

For example: (Pronunciation with syllables)

- Looked – (Lookd)
- Watched – (Watchd)
- Liked – (Likd)

Tip: For all words where Rule 2 applies, it is easier to think of the "d" as a "t" sound. For example, talked > (talkt)

Note: See how the "e" is not pronounced.

TOEFL Grammar Rule No.3 - *Present Perfect*

Description

The present perfect is used to say that an action happened at an unspecified time before now. The exact time is not important.

How To Use It

Structure: Have/has + past participle of the main verb

Example: "She has always spoken English", "I have never liked salad", "They have liked fish for a long time".

Explanation: You cannot use the present perfect with specific time expressions, like; yesterday, one year ago, last week, when I was a child, when I lived in Australia, at the moment, that day.

You can however use the present perfect with unspecific expressions, like; ever, never, once, many times, several times, before, already, etc.

The Basic Structure

Affirmative	Negative	Question
I <u>have</u> <u>been</u> to Spain	I <u>have</u> never/not <u>been</u> to Spain	<u>Have</u> you <u>been</u> to Spain?
She <u>has</u> <u>driven</u> a car	She <u>has</u> never/not <u>driven</u> a car	<u>Has</u> she <u>driven</u> a car?

When To Use It

Here are the two forms of when to use the present perfect:

1. An unspecified time before now.

For example: "I have seen that movie twenty times."
"People have not travelled to Mars."

2. Duration from the past until now (non-continuous verbs)

For example: "I have had a cold for two weeks.", "Mary has loved chocolate since she was a little girl."

Signal Words

The following words are commonly used with the Present Perfect.

<u>Ever:</u> Since you were born until right now.

<u>Just:</u> A few minutes ago. The action has completed recently.

<u>Already:</u> Is completed and now I´m doing something else.

<u>For:</u> Used to express a period of time (duration).

<u>Since:</u> Used to refer to the specific moment an action began.

TOEFL Grammar Rule No.4 - *Subject-Verb Agreement*

Description

The Subject - Verb agreement is an extremely important part of a sentence structure. The subject of a sentence must always "agree" with the verb that is being used in relation to that subject. In other words, the subject must match with the verb. A common mistake people make is when using plural or singular subjects.

When using a plural subject, the verb must be in the plural form and when using a singular subject, the verb must be in the singular form.

The table below explains this concept:

Singular	Plural
The employee <u>goes</u> to work	The employees <u>go</u> to work
The employee <u>is going</u> to work	The employees <u>are going</u> to work
The employee <u>has gone</u> to work	The employees <u>have gone</u> to work
The employee <u>went</u> to work	The employees <u>went</u> to work

How To Use It

The following steps will help you identify and use the appropriate subject and verb forms:

1. Identify the subject that is being used in the sentence
2. Determine whether the subject singular or plural form
3. Clarify which verb relates to which subject (sometimes there can be more than one subject)
4. Confirm that the correct verb conjugation corresponds with the subject

Let's firstly look at the Subject within a sentence.

Subjects:

Within a sentence, the subject will usually be a pronoun or noun.

As explained above, the subject (noun / pronoun) will either be in singular or plural form.

Most nouns can be changed into plural form by finishing the noun with an "s" or "es". However, some are irregular and don't have these endings, for example; man > men.

Regular Nouns

Singular	Plural
Table	Tables
Car	Cars
Plant	Plants

Irregular Nouns

Singular	Plural
Man	Men
Child	Children
Criterion	Criteria

Verbs:

Understanding if the verb is in singular form or plural form helps to confirm whether the subject should be in either singular form or plural form. The plural form can be made for most singular verbs in the "simple present" form by finishing the verb with an "s" or "es". However, this rule is only for regular verbs not irregular verbs.

When To Use It

You use the Subject-Verb agreement in just about every sentence you use. This is because just about every sentence has a subject and most times you are using verbs to provide information about the noun, which means the verb must agree with the noun.

Here are some examples with explanations:

She _____ her car yesterday.

    a) washed

    b) washes

    c) wash

    d) washer

A singular verb is required because "She" is also a subject in singular form. Answers (A) and (B) are singular verbs; however (A) is the correct answer because the tense of the sentence is in the simple past. The action occurred in the past from the word "yesterday", which means the verb must also be in the simple past tense.

The new employee and his manager _____ in an hour.

    a) arrives

    b) arrived

    c) has arrived

d) arrive

Because the subject of the sentence is two people (plural), the verb also must be plural. Therefore the correct answer is (D).

Important Tips

- The word "*Number*" as a combined noun can either be in a singular form or plural form. The verb will always be plural when the word "*a*" comes before the word "*number*", and the verb will always be singular when the word "*the*" comes before the word "*number*". (A **number** of people <u>feel</u> sick today / The **number** of employees <u>is</u> increasing.)

- A compound subject, two or more subjects joined by "*and*", takes a plural verb. (**Coffee and tea** <u>are</u> served hot.)

- A noun which is combined and names a group of things or people, although looks plural is actually one entity, which means it is singular. (The **group** <u>likes</u> the new task.)

- The verb always agrees with the closest part of a subject when the words "*or*" or "*nor*" are used between. This means if the verb will be in singular form if the closest part of the subject is also singular. The verb will be in plural form if the closest part of the subject is plural. (Neither the employee **nor** the manager <u>knows</u> the when the meeting will start.) (Either she **or** they <u>are</u> late.)

- The following words are always in singular form (Indefinite Pronouns):

- *anything, anyone, either, nothing, no one, neither, whoever, whatever, what, something, somebody, someone, everything, everyone, each, and everybody*

TOEFL Grammar Rule No.5 - *Negatives*

Description

"Negatives" are used to change the meaning of the verb from positive to negative, or state that something is not true or incorrect.

How To Use It

In order to claim that something is not true, you form a negative sentence by adding the word "NOT" after the first auxiliary verb in the positive sentence. If there is no auxiliary verb in the positive sentence, as in the Present Simple and Past Simple tenses, then you add one (in both these cases, the auxiliary verb "DO").

Note: When an auxiliary verb (including modals) is used, the main verb is not inflected (no "S" or "ED" ending), meaning that either the base form or past participle is used. The verb "TO BE" uses a different negation pattern.

Structure: The table below explains the structure.

Tense	Negative Element + Contracted Forms	Examples
Simple Present	Do + not = don't Does + not = doesn't	I do not play He doesn't play
Simple Past	Did + not = didn't	They didn't play
Present Continuous	Am + not Is + not = isn't Are + not = aren't	I am not playing She isn't playing We aren't playing
Past Continuous	Was + not = wasn't Were + not = haven't	I wasn't playing They weren't playing
Present Perfect	Have + never Have + not = haven't Has + never Has + not = hasn't	I have never played I haven't played She has never played She hasn't played
Future	Will + not = wont 'to be' + going to	I won't play I am not going to play

When To Use It

You use the "negative" form whenever you need to change the meaning to show that it is not true or incorrect.

TOEFL Grammar Rule No.6 - *Verb 'To Be' (Present / Past / Future)*

Description

The verb "to be" is one of the most used verbs in the English language. It is used in just about every sentence which means that you must learn how to use it correctly.

The verb "to be" is an Irregular verb and is used as the main verb for tense or as the auxiliary verb.

How To Use It

Structure: Pronoun + "to be" form + subject

The main verb is always the bare infinitive (infinitive without "to")

	Pronoun	'to be' form	Other
Affirmative	I	am	a student
Negative	He	is + not = isn't	a student
Question (Pronoun & 'to be' swap)	Are	they	students?

When To Use It

"To be" can be used the present, past and future; however

the form changes based on the tense.

Pronoun	'to be' form				Other
	Present	Past	Future	Present Perfect	
I	am	was	will be	have been	a student
You	are	were	will be	have been	a student
He/She/It	is	was	will be	has been	a student
We	are	were	will be	have been	a student
They	are	were	will be	have been	a student

TOEFL Grammar Rule No.7 - *Verb 'Can' (Present / Past / Future)*

Description

The verb "Can" is a modal/auxiliary verb that is used frequently in the English language. It is used to state opportunity or ability, to ask for or give consent, and to express possibility or impossibility.

How To Use It

Structure: Subject + "can" + main verb

The main verb must always be in the infinitive form, which means without "to".

	Subject	Auxiliary verb	Main verb	Other
Affirmative	I	can	play	tennis
Negative	He	cannot can't	play	tennis
Question	Can	you	play	tennis?

When To Use It

Can is used in the present, past and future; however the form changes based on the tense.

- Can / be able to (present)
- Could (past)
- Will be able to (future)

	Subject	Auxiliary verb	Main verb	Other
Present	I	can am able to	play	tennis
Past	I	could	play	tennis
Future	I	will be able to	play	tennis?

Important Tip

The main verb is ALWAYS the bare infinitive.

This is INCORRECT: "I can to play tennis."

TOEFL Grammar Rule No.8 - *Adverbs*

Description

Adverbs are words or phrases which describe verbs. In other words, Adverbs modify verbs by telling us "how" something is done.

How To Use It

Structure: Adjective + ly

Adjective	Adverb
Dangerous	Dangerously
Careful	Carefully
Nice	Nicely
Horrible	Horribly
Easy	Easily
Electronic	Electronically
Irregular Forms	
Good	Well
Fast	Fast
Hard	Hard

Rules:

When the adjective finishes in "y", change the "y" to "I". Then add "ly".

For example: Happy > happily

When the adjective finishes in "le", change the "le" to "ly".

For example: terrible > terribly

When the adjective finishes in "e", add "ly".

For example: Safe > safely

When To Use It

The examples below show when to use adverbs:

Adverbs of behaviour

- Slowly
- Kindly

Adverbs of quantity

- Very
- Rather

Adverbs of frequency

- Always
- Never

Adverbs of time

- Now
- Yesterday

Adverbs of location

- Here
- Somewhere

TOEFL Grammar Rule No.9 - *Adverbs of Frequency*

Description

Adverbs of frequency help to define how often or when an action is done.

The two types of adverbs of frequency are:

- Adverbs of "indefinite frequency"
- Adverbs of "definite frequency"

How To Use It

Adverbs of Infinite Frequency

Adverbs of indefinite frequency are different because they do not define the how many times an action occurs in a specific period of time.

Common examples are:

- very often
- usually
- always
- often
- never
- sometimes
- repeatedly
- rarely

- occasionally
- hardly ever
- typically

Adverbs of indefinite frequency are positioned within the central part of the sentence. The exact position is defined by the types of verbs used.

Below are the three sentence positions:

1. In between the noun/pronoun and the "main" verb.

For example:

- He **often** travels to the snow.
- The manager **always** starts works at 8am.
- The employees **usually** go out for lunch on Friday.

2. Following the verb "to <u>*be*</u>" but only if the verb is the "main" verb.

For example:

- She <u>is</u> **never** sick.
- The manager <u>is</u> **always** working late.
- The employees <u>are</u> **occasionally** early for work.

3. In between the "assisting" verb and the "main" verb, even if the "main" verb is a conjugated form of "to be".

For example:

- He has **never** travelled overseas.
- The managers can **often** finish work at 7pm.
- The director will **always** arrive before the employees.
- *Incorrect:* The students have been **often** disruptive.
- *Correct:* The students have **often** been disruptive. In this example the assisting verb is "have" and the main verb is "been".

Adverbs of Definite Frequency

Adverbs of definite frequency appear at the start or finish of a sentence. They describe exactly how many times the action happens within a specific period of time.

Common examples are:

- daily
- hourly
- monthly
- weekly
- yearly
- every day
- once a month

Examples of Adverbs of Definite Frequency:

- **Once a month**, the management team discuss logistics.
- Some workers arrive early **every day**.
- Timesheets are done **every week**.
- The operations manager has a meeting **daily**.

When To Use Them

You use adverbs of frequency when you need to provide more information about the verb you are using. Adverbs of frequency, when used correctly in speaking and writing and answered correctly in reading and listening, always help to increase your score.

TOEFL Grammar Rule No.10 - *This / That / These / Those*

Description

Demonstratives are used to explain how close the speaker is from other people, things, situations and experiences. In other words; the distance from the speaker.

How To Use Them

- THIS - used to describe a singular object that is close to the person speaking.
- THAT - used to describe a singular object that is far from the person speaking.
- THESE - used to describe plural objects that are close to the person speaking.
- THOSE - used to describe plural objects that are far from the person speaking.

	Singular	Plural	Close	Far
This	X	-	X	-
That	X	-	-	X
These	-	X	X	-
Those	-	X	-	X

When To Use Them

	Demonstratives	Demonstrative Adjectives
This	That is the place.	That restaurant is really good.
That	This is really good.	This book is really good.
These	These are a lot of fun.	These games are a lot of fun.
Those	Those are really good English books.	Those English books are really good.

TOEFL Grammar Rule No.11 - *Uncountable and Countable Nouns*

Description

Nouns take the form of being countable or uncountable.

Countable nouns are nouns that can be counted, which means they can take both the singular or plural form. On the other hand, uncountable nouns are unable to be counted because they are not individual and separate objects.

Uncountable nouns also cannot take the plural form because they cannot be counted and this means they are always singular. In addition, they never have the words "a" / "an" or a number in front of them.

How To Use Them

Countable - In front of a singular countable noun, use "a" / "an" or a number. For plural countable nouns, change the noun to plural form.

Uncountable – Use the uncountable noun on its own.

Countable	Uncountable
An apple / 1 apple	Rice
I eat an apple.	I eat rice every day. (INCORRECT > I eat a rice every day)
Apples are good for you.	Rice is good for you.

Uncountable nouns can be turned into countable nouns by adding a countable expression before the noun.

For example:

- A <u>piece</u> of information
- 2 <u>glasses</u> of water
- 10 <u>litres</u> of coffee

When To Use Them

To explain in simpler words, you use countable nouns when you can count the object but use uncountable nouns when you can't.

Words you can use with Countable and Uncountable nouns:

	Countable	Uncountable
Small quantity	A few / few	A little / little
Large quantity	Many / a lot (There are…)	A lot (There is…)
Questions	Many (Are there…?)	Much (Is there…?)
Negative	Many (There aren't…)	Much (There isn't…)

TOEFL Grammar Rule No.12 - *Comparisons*

Description

Comparisons are used to compare the differences or similarities between 2 or more objects.

To do this we can use adjectives in their comparative forms.

How To Use It

In order to use a comparison, you must take an adjective and change it based on a set of specific rules.

For example:

Adjective	Comparative	Superlative (the most)
Cold	Colder	Coldest

Structure: Here are the rules.

1. Adjectives with 1 or 2 syllables (that end in "Y" easy, "LE" gentle, "OW" shadow, "ET" quiet)

Comparative > "er"

Superlative > "est"

2. Adjectives with 2 syllables (that end in "Y" easy)

Comparative > "ier"

Superlative > "iest"

3. For all other 2 syllables and 3 syllables

Comparative > put the word "more" in front of the adjective (more exciting)

Superlative > put the word "most" in front of the adjective (most exciting)

Here are some exceptions to the rule:

Adjective	Comparative	Superlative
Good	Better than	The best
Bad	Worse than	The worst
Little	Less than	The least
Far	Farther than	The farthest
Many/Much	More than	The most

When To Use It

Comparatives – are used when you want to compare 2 or more objects.

For example: She is taller than him.

Superlatives – are used when you want to state that an object is the maximum or minimum of all objects.

For example: she is the tallest. She is the smallest.

TOEFL Grammar Rule No.13 - *Indefinite Pronouns*

Description

Indefinite pronouns are used as an unspecific description of the subject. This means that Indefinite Pronouns do not indicate a specific object, quantity or person. Because they are not definite, these pronouns usually take the third person form.

Indefinite Pronouns take either the singular or plural form. However, sometimes they can be singular situation and plural in another.

How To Use It

You simply replace the pronoun with the correct indefinite pronoun.

For example: "Peter is driving the car." > "Someone is driving the car."

Singular	Plural	Both
Another	Both	All
Anybody	Few	Any
Anything	Many	More

Each	Others	Most
Either	Several	None
Everybody		Some
Everyone		
Little		
Much		
Neither		
Nobody		
One		
Other		

When To Use It

You use Indefinite Pronouns when you either don't know who or what the object is or it is not necessary to state who or what the object is.

Important Tip

In English there can NEVER be two negatives in a sentence.

For example: "There isn't nobody." (INCORRECT) > "There isn't anybody." (CORRECT)

TOEFL Grammar Rule No.14 - *Conditional*

Description

There are three conditionals in English and each one has a specific use and form. Conditionals are used to describe possible circumstances or imaginary situations.

How To Use It

<u>First conditional</u> – This means that the situation is a possibility and quite likely that it will happen.

Structure: If + present simple, ... future simple (Will)

<u>Second conditional</u> – This means that it is a possibility but not very likely to happen.

Structure: If + past simple, ... would/could + infinitive

<u>Third conditional</u> – This means that is impossible to happen because it refers to the past.

Structure: If + past perfect, ... would + have + past participle

When To Use It

Examples of each conditional:

First conditional – "If I find my car keys, I will go to the movies."

Second conditional – "If I found my car keys, I would go to the movies."

Third conditional – "If I had found my car keys, I would have gone to the movies."

Example TOEFL writing question:

"If you were given a gift of money, what would you do with the money and why?."

TOEFL Grammar Rule No.15 - *Reported Speech*

Description

Reported Speech is reporting on the information from what other people say or think. This is done not by using the speaker's exact words but reported (indirect) speech.

When using reported speech you must also changes the tense to the past. This is because when you are describing what a person said, you are reporting on an action that happened in the past.

How To Use It

When you are reporting on something a person has said, you must use the tense previous to the person you are reporting about.

The tables below show the initial person talking about a situation (Direct Speech) and the person reporting (Reported Speech). The right column demonstrates that the person reporting must go back a tense.

Direct Speech	Reported Speech
Present simple She said, "it's cold"	*Past simple* "She said it was cold"
Present continuous She said, "I'm teaching English online"	*Past continuous* "She said she was teaching English online"
Past simple She said, "I taught online yesterday"	*Past perfect* "She said she had taught online yesterday"

Modal verb forms

Direct Speech	Reported Speech
Will She said, "I'll teach English online tomorrow"	*Would* "She said she would teach English online tomorrow"
Can She said, "I'll teach English online"	*Could* "She said she could teach English online"

When To Use It

In the TOEFL exam the most likely time to use Reported Speech is for the Integrated Speaking and Writing questions because these questions involve listening to a speaker and requiring you to report on what they said.

TOEFL Grammar Rule No.16 - *Used to*

Description

Used to indicates that a specific action was an old habit but has now stopped. It expresses the idea that the action was often occurred in the past, but does not usually happen now.

How To Use It

Below explains the difference between "used" and "use".

- When there is "did" in the sentence, we say "use to" (without "d")
- When there is no "did" in the sentence, we say "used to" (with "d")

Type	Subject	Auxiliary "did"	Not	Main Verb "use"	Infinitive
Affirmative	I			used	to do
Negative	I	did	not	use	to do
Question	Did	you		use	to do?

When To Use It

There are two uses for "used to".

1. Habit in the past

"Johnny used to study Spanish." (*He doesn't study it now*)

"Tim and Daniella used to go to Chile in the winter." (*They don't go there anymore*)

"I used to finish classes at 8 o'clock." (*I don't anymore*)

2. Past facts and generalisations

"I used to ride a motorbike."

"Sam used to be a chef, but now she is a layer."

"Jerry used to live in Spain, but now he lives in Australia."

TOEFL Grammar Rule No.17 - *Either / Neither / Both*

Description

Either and Neither are used in almost the same way as "so" and "too", but they are used with negative verbs. Both are used to explain that two subjects something in common.

How To Use It

<u>Both</u> = this AND that

- Used with the word "and"

<u>Either</u> = this OR that

- Goes at the end of the sentence after the negative helping verb

<u>Neither</u> = NOT this and NOT that

- Goes after the conjugation, the helping verb, and then the subject
- Neither has a negative connotation and therefore the sentence must not have another negative word
- Used with the word "nor"

When To Use It

Here are examples of when to use each form:

<u>Both</u>

"Emma and Megan both went to the party."

<u>Either</u>

"Do you want either chocolate or chips?"

"Max and Sophie are not going to either Spain or France."

<u>Neither</u>

"I like neither cats nor dogs."

"Neither Max nor Sophie is going to the party."

TOEFL Grammar Rule No.18 - *Transition Phrases or Words*

Description

Transition phrases allow your ideas and paragraphs to flow together. Without these transition phrases it is difficult to connect your ideas throughout your TOEFL writing and speaking answers.

How To Use Them

Transition phrases are generally used at the beginning of a sentence, but can also be used in the middle of a sentence depending on the type.

In order to use them correctly you need to think about "connection" between your sentences.

Here is a paragraph __without__ transition phrases:

"Australia is a country with many places to visit but can be very hot in the summer time. This does not stop many people from coming to enjoy its attractions."

Here is a paragraph <u>with</u> transition phrases:

"<u>Even though</u> Australia is a country with many places to visit, it can be very hot in the summer. <u>However,</u> this does not stop many people from coming to Australia to enjoy its attractions.

As you can see above, the two transition phrases are used to help the reader and direct them with what the following sentence is about and helping connect the information together easier.

When To Use Them

In order to achieve a high score on the TOEFL, you MUST use transition phrases.

Here are examples of phrases to use for different purposes:

<u>Introduction</u>

- "Firstly…"
- "Secondly…"
- "In my opinion…"
- "There are two reasons why…"

Supporting points

- "On the other hand..."
- "For example..."
- "In contrast..."
- "However..."
- "In fact..."
- "In addition..."

Conclusion

- "Therefore..."
- "As a result..."
- "In conclusion..."

"And" Group

- "Too (end of sentences)"
- "As well as..."
- "Furthermore..."
- "Both... and..."

"But" Group

- "Through..."
- "Although..."
- Nevertheless..."
- On the other hand..."

"So" Group

- "As a result…"
- "Therefore…"
- "Consequently…"

TOEFL Grammar Rule No.19 - *Other / Another*

Description

Another and Other are two commonly used words in the English language but can easily be confused.

- <u>Another</u> – is used with singular nouns.
- <u>Other</u> – is used for both singular and plural or uncountable nouns.

How To Use Them

Structure: <u>Another</u> + singular countable noun

Example:

- "Let's have <u>another</u> hamburger." [hamburger = countable, singular]
- "Can I eat <u>another</u> orange?" [orange = countable, singular]

Note: Another is used for an additional person or thing of the same kind.

Structure: <u>Other</u> + plural or uncountable noun

Example:

- "<u>Other</u> cities are bigger than mine." [cities = plural noun]
- "This shop sells <u>other</u> bread." [bread = uncountable noun]

Note: Other refers to all people or things that are not the particular one being mentioned.

Note: The word "Others" cannot be used as the plural of the word "Other". "Other" can be used as a pronoun or adjective, but "others" must always be a pronoun.

- "Jonny attended the class with nine <u>other</u> students." [adjective]
- "Some teachers are better at explaining things than <u>others</u>." [pronoun]

When To Use It

- <u>Another</u> – when you want the same of one thing.

- <u>Other</u> – when you are talking about nonspecific singular or plural things different to the one being mentioned.

TOEFL Grammar Rule No.20 - *Passive Voice*

Description

The Passive voice is a highly recommended form to use for more formal situations; like a formal letter.

The Passive voice is commonly used when the attention needs to be more on the "action", instead of who or what is doing the action.

How To Use It

Structure: Who/What receiving action + be + past participle of verb + by + Who/What doing action

Tense	Active Voice	Passive Voice
Simple Present	Once a week, Tom cleans the house.	Once a week, the house is cleaned by Tom.
Past Simple	Sam repaired the car.	The car was repaired by Sam.
Present Perfect	Many tourists have visited that castle	That castle has been visited by many tourists.
Simple Future	Someone will finish the work by 5:00pm.	The work will be finished by 5:00pm.

When To Use It

You must use the passive voice in your writing and speaking answers in the TOEFL.

This is because the passive voice is seen by TOEFL evaluators as a more formal form of presenting the information, whereas the Active voice is seen as a simpler form, hence the Passive voice will attract a higher TOEFL score.

TOEFL Grammar Rule No.21 - *Prepositions*

Description

Prepositions are words that are usually placed in front of nouns and sometimes in front of verbs in gerund form.

They are used to guide the reader and help them understand what the writer is trying to say.

Prepositions are difficult because a preposition in your native language could have several different meanings in English. The best way is to simply learn them and practice them.

How To Use Them

Prepositions are split into Time and Place (position and direction).

Prepositions – Time

Preposition	Use	Example
On	Days of the week	On Monday
In	Month Time of day Year	In August In the morning In 2006
At	Night	At night

	Weekend	At the weekend
Since	From a certain point of time	Since 1980
For	Over a certain period of time	For 2 years
Ago	A certain time in the past	3 years ago
Before	Earlier than a certain point of time	Before 2003
To	Telling the time	Ten to six (5:50)
Past	Telling the time	15 past six (6:15)

Prepositions – Place (position and direction)

Preposition	Use	Example
In	Room, building, town Book Car World	In the kitchen In the book In the car In the world
At	For table For events Place where you do typical things	At the table At the concert At the cinema
On	Attached On a surface For public transport	The picture on the wall On the table On the bus

	For television	On TV
Next to	Left or right of something	Jane is standing next to the car
Under	Lower than something else	The bag is under the table
Below	Lower than something else but above ground	The table is below the painting
Over	Covered by something	Put a jacket over your shirt
Above	Higher than something else but not directly over it	A path above the lake
Across	Getting to the other side	Walk across the bridge
From	In the sense of "where from"	A flower from the garden

TOEFL Grammar Rule No.22 - *Parallelism*

Description

Parallelism is the matching or continuation of grammar structures within a sentence. Parts of a sentence which express similar ideas within a sentence must be grammatically parallel or match each other so the sentence is balanced. Parallelism prevents the sentence from being awkward and increases clarity and improves readability.

How To Use It

There needs to be balance between the elements of a sentence, whether they are nouns, verb tenses, prepositional phrases, comparisons or conjunctions.

Nouns

- Nouns must balance with other nouns in the sentence. For example, "I enjoy soccer more than playing rugby". The problem is that "soccer" is a noun, but "playing rugby" is a phrase. The correct form should use "soccer" and "rugby".

Verb Tense

- Verb tenses also need to be balanced. There is something incorrect with this sentence: "Yesterday, I went to class, cooked and was listening to music."

  The last element used, has a different verb tense than the first two; all verb tenses must be the same. For example, "Yesterday, I went to class, cooked and *listened* to music."

Prepositional Phrases

- Prepositional phrases must also balance with other prepositional phrases. For example, "Next week we can go out for dinner and eating ice cream". The prepositional phrase "out for dinner" is not parallel with the verb "eating." The correct sentence is: "Next week we can go out for dinner and eat ice cream."

Comparing

- Comparisons commonly use words like; "than" or "as". When using a comparison, make sure the subjects being compared are in parallel. This sentence is incorrect: "Riding my bike to school is as quick as the train." This sentence is correct: "Riding my bike to school is as fast as taking the train."

Conjunctions

- Correlative conjunctions such as "either...or", "both...and," or "rather...than," must also have parallel items. This sentence is incorrect: "John wants both happiness and healthy." This sentence is correct: "John wants both happiness and health."

When To Use It

You must use parallelism when you are developing sentences using the above contexts.

TOEFL Grammar Rule No.23 - *Pronoun Reference*

Description

Pronoun Reference is where a pronoun takes the place of a noun. When this occurs, the pronoun should clearly refer to one, unmistakable noun which comes before the pronoun. This noun is called the antecedent.

Pronouns must agree with their antecedent and the relationship must be very clear and unmistakable.

How To Use It

When replacing a word by a pronoun, make sure there is a coherent relationship between them, this refers to: gender, number etc. If the pronoun does not have a clear antecedent, the reader can become confused.

The following are typical mistakes when using Pronoun Reference:

Mistake No. 1 – Too many antecedents

Example: *"The student's mother felt upset when she received a "D" in mathematics."*

In this case, "*she*" is replacing either "*mother*" or "*the student*". However, it is not clear which noun is being replaced since both can be a singular feminine noun.

Solution: Do not use a pronoun; instead use the noun.

Correct: *"The student's mother felt upset when the student received a "D" in mathematics."*

Mistake No. 2 – No antecedent

Example: *"The lady called the hospital, but they didn't answer."*

In this case, "they" does not have a noun antecedent which it refers to.

Solution: Use the noun or insert an antecedent that clearly refers to the pronoun.

Correct: *"The lady called the hospital, but the receptionists didn't* answer."

Or

Correct: *"The lady called the hospital receptionists, but they didn't answer."*

BONUS - *TOEFL Grammar Exercises*

Choose the correct alternative for each sentence. Check the answers at the end of this section.

1) The Prime Minister _____ to make a quick decision.

(A) needs

(B) needing

(C) need

(D) needed

2) My teacher _____ me how to use the Simple Past yesterday in class.

(A) teached

(B) taught

(C) teaches

(D) teach

3) I _____ in this company for two years.

(A) have worked

(B) worked

(C) has worked

(D) working

4) The students' mother _____ very upset about her children's behaviour

(A) been

(B) were

(C) was

(D) being

5) Citizens _____ decided who to vote for in the next elections.

(A) hasn't

(B) wasn't

(C) weren't

(D) haven't

6) Tomorrow _____ a very rainy and windy day.

(A) is

(B) will be

(C) was

(D) be

7) I'm sorry, I _____ help you with your homework tomorrow, I'll be busy.

(A) won't able to

(B) am not able to

(C) wasn't able to

(D) being able to

8) After the accident, the witness _____ called the police to get help.

(A) quick

(B) quicker

(C) quickly

(D) quickest

9) My classmate _____ late for class.

(A) always be

(B) always is

(C) be always

(D) is always

10) We are all equal and free. _____ are undeniable rights stated in our constitution.

(A) This

(B) These

(C) That

(D) Those

11) _____ students _____ in class today?

(A) How much – is there

(B) How many – is there

(C) How much – are there

(D) How many – are there

12) Commuting by train is _____ than by doing it by bus.

(A) much faster

(B) much more fast

(C) much fast

(D) much fastest

13) _____ broke into the apartment and stole US $3000.

(A) somebody

(B) everybody

(C) nobody

(D) anybody

14) I know that if I _____ hard, I _____ get the TOEFL score I need.

(A) studies – would

(B) study – will

(C) studied – will

(D) study – would

15) Peter _____ buy a sports car if he _____ the lottery.

(A) will – wins

(B) would – won

(C) would – wins

(D) will – win

16) If Sarah _____ how hard this class was, she _____ it.

(A) knew – wouldn't take

(B) has known – wouldn't take

(C) had known – wouldn't have taken

(D) had known – wouldn't has taken

17) Anna said that she _____ that mistake again.

(A) would never make

(B) is never make

(C) isn't ever making

(D) never is making

18) My mother _____ a lullaby before going to bed every night.

(A) use to sang

(B) used to sang

(C) use to sing

(D) used to sing

19) _____ Sam ____ Tom _____ going to the conference tomorrow.

(A) either – or – are

(B) neither – or – is

(C) either – nor – is

(D) neither – nor – is

20) _____, studies have shown a negative increase in the levels of obesity worldwide _____ all the efforts made to reduce this global problem.

(A) Recently – however

(B) Recently – in spite of

(C) Seriously – but

(D) Later – due to

21) The president said we need _____ policies to solve the problems in economy, otherwise _____ crisis will affect the country.

(A) others – other

(B) other – others

(C) other – another

(D) others – another

22) Twenty people _____ after the student protests held yesterday.

(A) have been arrested

(B) has been arrested

(C) have been arrest

(D) has been arrest

23) The book was _____ the shelf but it just fell ____ and now it is _____ the drawer.

(A) in – from – on

(B) on – off – in

(C) on – from – in

(D) in – off– on

24) Mr Smith is one of the best teachers I have had, not only is he a good professional, but also _____.

(A) qualified

(B) has qualifications

(C) a qualified individual

(D) a qualification individual

25) Ms. Simms told Bob's associate that _____ had written a fine report.

(A) Bob's associate

(B) she

(C) he

(D) Bob

ANSWER KEY

1) A

2) B

3) A

4) C

5) D

6) B

7) A

8) C

9) D

10) B

11) D

12) A

13) A

14) B

15) B

16) C

17) A

18) D

19) D

20) B

21) C

22) A

23) B

24) C

25) A

About The Author

Tim Dickeson

Tim is a highly sought after TOEFL consultant due to his ability to "translate the complexities of the TOEFL into a simple language".

His simplified but highly effective approach to TOEFL preparation has proven time after time that his methods get results.

Tim is Australian born and raised and has taught English and TOEFL in Australia, Europe and South America. He currently owns a TOEFL preparation company in South America and has consulted for universities and language institutions about how to correctly prepare people for the TOEFL iBT.

He has a love of teaching and helping people achieve results and his number one objective with the TOEFL High Score System is to help as many people as possible pass the TOEFL so they can continue to pursue their dreams.